Before They Were Famous

Babe Ruth

Written by Stephen Krensky
Illustrated by Bobbie Houser

A Crabtree Crown Book

Crabtree Publishing
crabtreebooks.com

School-to-Home Support for Caregivers and Teachers

This book is designed to teach and appeal to a student on core subject areas. The student will build upon what they already know about the subject and engage in topics that they do not know but want to learn more about. Here are a few guiding questions to help the reader on his or her comprehension skills. Possible answers appear here in red.

Before Reading:

What do I know about this topic?

- *I know that Babe Ruth is considered the best baseball player of all time.*
- *I know that Babe Ruth was well known for the many home runs he hit during his baseball career.*

What do I want to learn about this topic?

- *I want to learn more about the kind of trouble George, later nicknamed Babe, got into as a young boy.*
- *I want to learn more about the achievements Babe Ruth made while playing baseball.*

During Reading:

I'm curious to know...

- *I'm curious to know how Babe Ruth did in his classes at school.*
- *I'm curious to know if Babe Ruth ever got in trouble with law enforcement.*

How is this like something I already know?

- *I know that some great athletes are terrific students while others struggle with their studies.*
- *I know that sometimes people make bad choices that lead them to jail.*

After Reading:

What was the author trying to teach me?

- *I think the author was trying to teach me that you must have perseverance and never quit when you have a dream for yourself to achieve great things.*
- *I think the author was trying to teach me that although you may come from a poor family you can achieve great things in life.*

How did the photographs and captions help me understand more?

- *I didn't know that Babe Ruth was only 19 years old when he received his first contract to play professional baseball.*
- *I didn't know that Babe Ruth was a great pitcher for the Red Sox in his early career.*

Table of Contents

Sent Away

The seven-year-old boy stared up and up and up. A five-story tall building stood in front of him. Other smaller buildings sat nearby, and they were all surrounded by a tall wall. The gray stone looked firm and **fierce**. And maybe a little scary.

The name of the place was *St. Mary's* **Industrial** *School for Boys*. It sounded a little scary, too.

DELINQUENT

St. Mary's was a home for orphans, as well as **delinquent** boys.

ORPHANAGE

Early Facts

St. Mary's had opened in 1866 and remained open until 1950.

Little George Herman Ruth, Jr., wasn't actually an orphan. But he was delinquent and wayward, and his parents no longer thought they could take charge of him. "**Incorrigible**" was the word often used to describe his behavior.

Early Facts

Young George rarely saw his family after he moved, and his mother died when he was twelve.

"BAD" BOY

The Orphanage

The Ruth family lived in a part of Baltimore, Maryland, called Pigtown. It had earned that name because hundreds of pigs were often herded through the streets from a **stockyard** to a **slaughterhouse** nearby.

Babe Ruth Birthplace and Museum at 216 Emory Street.

George spent most of his time on the street getting into mischief. He stole apples and eggs — and sometimes he ate them. Other times he threw them at people passing by.

Sadly, George's parents didn't have the time or the patience to deal with George. And so, they had made the big decision to send him away.

"I was a bum when I was a kid," George later recalled.

Early Facts

The Ruths had eight children, but only George, Jr., the firstborn, and his younger sister Mary survived to adulthood.

Many of the 800 boys at St. Mary's came from difficult backgrounds. And the school was happy to accept them, but the rules were strict. The boys were roused at 6:00 a.m. sharp, and the lights were turned off promptly at 8:00 p.m.

Fun Facts

The children at St. Mary's ranged in age from five to 21.

In between those hours, the boys got an education. They were also taught skills in case their future jobs depended more on trade skills than reading and writing.

George learned how to make shirts and also to handle a hammer and saw. If he ended up pursuing a career as a carpenter, he would be prepared.

Fun Facts

In later years George would make adjustments to his own shirt collars even though he could afford to have a tailor do them.

A Sporting Chance

But not everything at St. Mary's was about school and work. There was also time for sports, especially baseball. One of the teachers, **Brother** Matthias, saw **potential** in George. He spent hours teaching the young boy how to hit and field the ball.

Although George was a lefty, the school had no left-handed baseball gloves. So, Brother Matthias gave him a right-handed catcher's mitt. Even though it was uncomfortable, George wore the glove on his right hand so that he could still throw with his left.

Brother Matthias

BASEBALL

Fun Facts

The earliest rules of baseball date from 1845. They were written for a New York City club called the Knickerbockers.

It was soon clear that George's baseball skills were more advanced than even the older boys. He was just a natural at throwing and catching. And no one could match him for walloping the ball.

Sometimes, though, George wasn't very nice about players who were not as good as he was. One day, when a pitcher was having a tough outing, George made fun of him.

Fun Facts

Ruth began his baseball career in what was known as the Dead Ball era because games tended to be low scoring. In 1921, scores suddenly increased with new pitching rules and changes to the ball.

Brother Matthias immediately stopped the game. He thought, if George had so much to say, he must think he could do better. In that case, he felt he should go out and pitch himself.

Now.

And then Brother Matthias handed him the ball.

Making a Pitch

Everyone on both teams stared at George. He had no idea how to pitch, but he couldn't refuse Brother Matthias. And so, George trudged out to the mound.

Fun Facts

In the history of baseball, only twenty-three pitchers have thrown a perfect game in which no batter ever gets on base.

GAME DAY

But on his first pitch, he discovered something. George could actually throw the ball hard and fast. "As soon as I got out there," he later recalled, "I felt a strange relationship with the pitcher's mound. It was as if I'd been born out there. Pitching just felt like the most natural thing in the world."

After that, George practiced pitching as much as hitting and fielding. There was a lot to learn from Brother Matthias. Depending on how George gripped the ball, he could make it do different things on the way to home plate. Throwing it really hard was only helpful if the ball stayed in the **strike zone**.

Babe Ruth - St. Mary's Industrial School 1912.

Fun Facts

In Ruth's era, the fastest pitches were thrown about 90 miles per hour (145 kph) compared to over 100 miles an hour (160 kph) today.

The Big Leagues

Before long George was being written up in the Baltimore newspapers for his baseball success. Hitting, fielding, pitching — not only could George do them all, he was also the best at all three.

Fun Facts

These Baltimore Orioles, part of a minor league, had no relationship with the current major league Baltimore Orioles, who adopted the same name in 1953.

A little while later, Jack Dunn, the owner of the minor-league Baltimore Orioles, came to see George work out. Dunn watched George for less than an hour. Then he offered him a contract to play baseball.

Jack Dunn

George was only nineteen years old. He had never thought about baseball as a job. But compared to his other options, it seemed like an exciting thing to try.

As a new player, or rookie, George was teased a lot at baseball practice. But the veteran players were warned to be careful about that. The coaches knew that Mr. Dunn cared a lot about George. He was one of Dunn's "babes," young and inexperienced, but with a whole lot of potential.

Fun Facts

As a rookie with the Red Sox, Babe once found his bats had been sawed in half by veteran players after he tried to take batting practice with the established players.

Even so, baseball was still a business. So, when the chance came a few months later to sell his young player, by now known as Babe Ruth, to the major-league Boston Red Sox, Jack Dunn did just that.

On July 11, 1914, Babe Ruth pitched his first game for the Boston Red Sox against the Cleveland Indians. He actually struck out in his first time at bat. But as he said later, "Never let the fear of striking out get in your way."

Fun Facts

It was less than six months after he left St. Mary's that Babe Ruth began pitching for the Boston Red Sox.

Babe Ruth and other Red Sox Pitchers, 1915.

Babe's first home run came almost a year later. His career was quickly taking off — even faster than that home run ball. And there would be no turning back. As he said later, "I swing big with everything I've got. I hit big or I miss big. I like to live as big as I can."

Fun Facts

Taking his pitching and hitting statistics together, Babe Ruth continues to be considered the greatest baseball player of all time.

New York

George Herman Ruth, Jr., was born on February 6th, 1895. Although he first gained attention as a pitcher, his powerful hitting soon earned him other positions on days he wasn't pitching.

In perhaps the most famous trade in the history of baseball, Boston Red Sox owner Harry Frazee sold Babe Ruth to the New York Yankees in December 1919. Known as The Babe, The Sultan of Swat, and The Bambino, he enjoyed his glory years with the Yankees, winning seven American League championships and four World Series. And his record total of 714 home runs lasted until 1974.

In 1936, Babe Ruth was one of the first three baseball players to be elected to the new Baseball Hall of Fame. He died after a long battle with cancer on August 16, 1948. Over 100,000 people came to pay their respects at his funeral.

GLOSSARY

Brother
A religious title for a man who belongs to a religious community

delinquent
A young person who often commits minor crimes

fierce
Showing intense energy and sometimes inspiring fear

incorrigible
A person's behavior, which cannot be corrected or reformed

industrial
Having to do with skills in a trade

potential
Showing the ability to develop greater success or achievement with specific skills

slaughterhouse
A place where animals are killed and cut up into pieces as food

stockyard
A large fenced-in yard where livestock are gathered

INDEX

COMPREHENSION QUESTIONS

What was the full name of the school where George was sent to live as a boy?

What was the name of George's teacher who taught him so much about baseball?

What was the first professional baseball team that George played for?

ABOUT THE AUTHOR

Stephen Krensky is the award-winning author of more than 150 fiction and nonfiction books for children. He and his wife Joan live in Lexington, Massachusetts, and he happily spends as much time as possible with his grown children and not-so-grown grandchildren.

Written by: Stephen Krensky
Illustrations by: Bobbie Houser
Designed by: Bobbie Houser
Series Development: James Earley
Proofreader: Kathy Middleton
Educational Consultant: Marie Lemke M.Ed.
Production manager: Candice Campbell

Photographs: t = Top, c = Center, b = Bottom, l = Left, r = Right

Alamy: History and Art Collection: p. 5 c; Wim Wiskerke: p. 8 r; Amoret Tanner: p. 10 c; Science History Images: p. 11 tl; Social History Images: p. 11 br; Everett Collection: p. 12 c; Wolverhampton Archives, UK: p. 13 t; CHARLES PHELPS CUSHING: p. 14 b; Archivah: p. 21 t, 27 b; The Protected Art Archive: p. 23 l; PictureLux: p. 25 r; Pictorial Press: p. 26 r; The History Collection: p. 28 l; Library of Congress: cover bl, p. 29 br; Shutterstock: Andiz.od: cover tl; Palokha Tetiana: cover br, p. 14 tr; Tetyana Afanasyeva: p. 4 bl; Tomasz Guzowski: p. 5 t; Artist_R: p. 5 bl; alicedaniel: p. 6 l; Stuart Monk: p. 6 r; marekuliasz: p. 7 t; Alexander_P: p. 7 br; JosepPerianes: p. 8 tl; Sunny_nsk: p. 8 bl; Photoexpert: p. 9 l; Volodymyr Burdiak: p. 10 r; dmitroscope: p. 11 tr; Lemon Workshop Design: p. 11 bl; mishu: p. 12 br; AVA Bitter: p. 13 cl; enterlinedesign: p. 15 c, 19 tr; Mtrisma: p. 15 bl; squarelogo: p. 16 tr; lalilele13: p. 16 br, 18 br; Alluvion Stock: p. 17 tr; Bankrx: p. 18 cl; ExpertOutfit: p. 21 br; Mile Atanasov: p. 21 br; fifg: p. 22 bl, 29 tr; RetroClipArt: p. 22 tr; eurobanks: p. 23 br; Emilia Dragomir: p. 24 tr; pterwort: p. 24 c; DELstudio: p. 24 bl; JosepPerianes: p. 25 tl; Alexander Varbenov: p. 25 bl; Baka Sobaka: p. 26 l; p. 27 tl; CiEll: p. 27 tr; skizer: p. 28 r; TanyaFox: p. 29 tl; Society for American Baseball Research: p. 15 tr

Crabtree Publishing

crabtreebooks.com 800-387-7650

Printed in the U.S.A./CP072026

Published in Canada Crabtree Publishing
616 Welland Ave.
St. Catharines, Ontario
L2M 5V6

Published in the United States Crabtree Publishing
347 Fifth Ave
Suite 1402-145
New York, NY 10016

Library and Archives Canada Cataloguing in Publication
Available at Library and Archives Canada

Library of Congress Cataloging-in-Publication Data
Available at the Library of Congress

Hardcover: 978-1-0398-3888-8
Paperback: 978-1-0398-3973-1
Ebook (pdf): 978-1-0398-4048-5
Epub: 978-1-0398-4120-8